# TDD by example
## Evaluating an expression

MARCEL POPESCU

This publication is licensed under a Creative Commons Attribution 3.0 Unported License, available at
http://creativecommons.org/licenses/by/3.0/

You can contact the author at mdpopescu@renfieldsoftware.com

Cover image: Simon Howden / FreeDigitalPhotos.net

# CONTENTS

| | |
|---|---|
| Chapter 1. Rationale and preparation | 7 |
|     1.1. Why TDD? | 7 |
|     1.2. Preparation | 11 |
| Chapter 2. First acceptance tests | 13 |
|     2.1. Unit tests | 14 |
|     2.2. Addition | 21 |
|     2.3. Subtraction | 22 |
|     2.4. Refactoring | 23 |
|     2.5. Parsing | 25 |
|     2.6. Extracting a new class | 28 |
|     2.7. Operators | 30 |
| Chapter 3. More operations | 42 |
|     3.1. Refactoring | 46 |
|     3.2. Division | 48 |
|     3.3. Refactoring | 50 |
|     3.4. Mocking | 57 |
|     3.5. More dependencies | 60 |
| Chapter 4. Multiple operations | 63 |
|     4.1. Smells-driven refactoring | 65 |
|     4.2. Lists | 68 |
|     4.3. Operator precedence | 75 |
| Chapter 5. More complex expressions | 78 |
|     5.1. Negative numbers | 78 |
|     5.2. Parentheses | 82 |
|     5.3. Refactoring | 88 |
| Chapter 6. Floating-point numbers | 89 |
|     6.1. Malformed expressions | 96 |
|     6.2. Spaces | 99 |
| Chapter 7. Symbols | 100 |
| Chapter 8. Conclusion | 104 |

# Chapter 1. Rationale and preparation

## 1.1. Why TDD?

It is said that the best way to learn something is to teach someone else; this is my attempt at teaching others test-driven design (hereafter TDD) in order to deepen my own understanding of it. In addition, I had often wished – at the beginning of my journey into programming – to read a book that would show how another programmer thinks and works through his or her mistakes. Just like in science or mathematics, where sometimes it is more interesting to find out how the law or theorem was reached, so it is in programming; yes, that is a nice program, with a clean design – but how did it get that way?

Finding a subject was a problem for me; there are two opposite forces, as it were – I need something simple enough that I can focus on the TDD process instead of the actual problem to be solved, but I also need something complex enough so that it doesn't get dismissed as a toy. In this book, I have settled on something that I found moderately difficult in the first years of programming – evaluating a mathematical expression. It would be great if you had tried solving this problem before – this way you can compare the approaches; but even if you didn't, I hope you can understand how the TDD process works and, as importantly, why it's useful.

In fact – why is TDD useful? I'll start by answering something else: why is automated testing useful? Donald Knuth famously said "Beware of bugs in the above code; I have only proved it correct, not tried it."[1] We need to test the code, if only for psychological reasons; the feeling of "I've made something that works" is a great motivator for all the programmers I know.

If we agree that testing is necessary, automated testing is almost a given; we're programmers, we like automating stuff. Testing is something that needs to be done frequently – otherwise we risk fixing a bug in one place only to cause three to pop up in other places. Since manually testing every bit of code is difficult to do (and boring), we need a testing framework to automate it.

Ok, testing is good; automated testing is better; why test before writing the code, though? How does that help? It helps because software is complex and well-designed software hard to get. It is often not hard to write the code to solve an immediate problem; writing the code that can solve that problem but is also flexible enough to allow us to quickly respond to changing requirements is more difficult. A good design helps code be flexible; test-driven design attempts to ensure that we have a good design at all times.

Why does TDD help to obtain a good design? In my experience, it helps to think of it not as writing tests, but as writing specifications; more importantly, as executable, non-ambiguous specifications. The fact that you must write the specifications before the code helps clarify your intent; the fact that you must write code that can be tested helps to make it less coupled. As you progress, the second part – having to write testable code – grows in importance because it creates

---

[1] http://www-cs-faculty.stanford.edu/~knuth/faq.html

"pain points": the parts of the code that are hard to test show you a problem with the code, a violation of a design principle.

Here's an example; you are writing code for a blog and you have a feature to implement: a method to show the posts older than a month. Easy:

```
private BlogDB db;

public IEnumerable<Post> GetOldPosts()
{
   return db
     .Posts
     .Where(post => post.DateTime < DateTime.Now.AddMonths(-1));
}
```

How do you test this? Since your method reads directly from the database, you will have to add several posts to it at the beginning of the test and then delete them at the end, so that you leave the database in the same state as it was before. The test is slow but, more importantly, any bug in it will create problems in the database – either leaving fictive posts in it or deleting real ones.

It is not the case that such a test cannot be written; it is, however, painful to run, which suggests that something needs to be done. In this particular case, extracting the db.Posts expression as a PostRepository interface that gets passed to our class in the constructor is one possible solution. The tests can now mock the interface and run completely in memory without touching the database; this eliminates both problems mentioned above and, in addition, creates a design that is less coupled: the class no longer depends on (needs to know about) the database directly, but instead depends on an abstraction.

*We have just re-discovered the Dependency Inversion Principle, which states:*

*1. High-level modules should not depend on low-level modules. Both should depend on abstractions.*

*2. Abstractions should not depend upon details. Details should depend upon abstractions.*

Let's continue; I have changed the code to look like this:

```
private PostRepository posts;

public IEnumerable<Post> GetOldPosts()
{
   return posts
     .Get()
     .Where(post => post.DateTime < DateTime.Now.AddMonths(-1));
}
```

There is still a dependency on a detail here, a concrete implementation: it is the dependency on the DateTime static class. This forces us to create fictive posts that depend on the date/time when the test is run, which creates the potential of non-reproducible failures (think about leap years for example). I should extract this dependency as an interface:

```
public interface Clock
{
   DateTime GetCurrentTime();
}
```

The method will change to:

```
private Clock clock;

public IEnumerable<Post> GetOldPosts()
{
   return posts
     .Get()
```

```
        .Where(post => post.DateTime <
clock.GetCurrentTime().AddMonths(-1));
    }
```

Now I can use hardcoded DateTime values in the test, making it run deterministically.

Note that, besides making the class easier to test, the above steps helped with something very important: it has exposed the dependencies. This class needs a post repository of some sort, as well as a clock; those dependencies were hidden before. That is never a good thing.[2]

This is one example of how TDD helps to obtain a cleaner design; I will discuss other "code smells" as they occur. However, there is one important point to make: TDD is not a panacea, a silver bullet. Some of the design changes will be guided by the tests; some of them will be guided by design principles; some by my experience. There's no one best design. TDD is just another weapon in your arsenal as a programmer.

## 1.2. Preparation

I have used Visual Studio 2010 and the MSTest testing framework to write this book; changing the code to use another testing framework like NUnit or xUnit should not be very difficult, as all the major concepts are the same. I also recommend using the Resharper add-on to Visual Studio; it makes life much easier.

This is a code-heavy book. Just reading it won't help you much; you have to follow it by writing the code. In order to do

---

[2] Miško Hevery has a great article on this at http://misko.hevery.com/2009/02/19/constructor-injection-vs-setter-injection/

that, you will have to create two projects: a class library with the actual evaluator (I've called it Math.ExpressionEvaluator) and a test project (which I've called Math.ExpressionEvaluator.Tests). You will also need the Moq framework, but I'll show you how to get it when the time comes.

## Chapter 2. First acceptance tests

When can the first version of the application be deployed? The minimal feature set, as it were? This is, of course, subjective and will vary wildly depending on the actual problem you're trying to solve; however, I suggest that you spend a few minutes thinking about the minimal version that can nevertheless be useful to a potential customer. In my opinion, it is better to err on the side of less instead of more features – it's better to get something out fast, so that the real customers can give you feedback.

For this particular problem – an expression evaluator – I am the customer; I have decided that adding and subtracting two integer numbers is good enough for a first version. Let's write an acceptance test for that.

I begin by adding an AcceptanceTests class to the Tests project:

```
[TestClass]
public class AcceptanceTests
{
}
```

followed by adding the first two tests:

```
[TestMethod]
public void CanAddTwoIntegerNumbers()
{
   var sut = new Evaluator();

   var result = sut.Eval("10+25");

   Assert.AreEqual(35, result);
}

[TestMethod]
public void CanSubtractTwoIntegerNumbers()
{
```

```
    var sut = new Evaluator();

    var result = sut.Eval("300-5");

    Assert.AreEqual(295, result);
}
```

As you can see, I have decided to call the main class *Evaluator*, and the method being called to evaluate the expression *Eval*. Not the best names, I admit but, as the saying goes, naming is one of the two hard problems in programming[3].

I am also using the variable *sut* to hold the new instance – from *system under test*. It's just a convention I'm using; feel free to call it anything else.

## *2.1. Unit tests*

Back to the acceptance tests; they will fail if I try to compile the code, obviously, so I will use them as guidelines to create my *unit tests*. I don't want to write production code that is not first guarded by unit tests – or, to put it another way, I don't want to write production code without first writing executable *specifications*. Therefore, I create another class and call it EvaluatorTests (by convention, I'm going to call all unit tests for class X *XTests*):

```
[TestClass]
public class EvaluatorTests
{
}
```

What is the simplest requirement I can come up with for this problem? I can think of two: an empty (or null) string should

---

[3] http://www.tbray.org/ongoing/When/200x/2005/12/23/UPI

throw an exception; a one-digit number should return its value. The first one is simpler so I write it:

```
[TestMethod]
[ExpectedException(typeof (Exception))]
public void NullOrEmptyStringThrowsException()
{
   var sut = new Evaluator();

   sut.Eval("");
}
```

This test is still not compiling, but now I can write the actual code to fix that:

```
public class Evaluator
{
   public int Eval(string s)
   {
      return 0;
   }
}
```

Everything compiles, including the acceptance tests, so I run the tests (press the second toolbox button, Run All Tests in Solution, or use the Ctrl-R, A shortcut). The two acceptance tests are predictably failing; we're going to ignore them for now. More importantly, the unit test fails with the message "...did not throw expected exception System.Exception."

Good. The test fails exactly as it should – the method being called is supposed to do something and it doesn't. Easy to fix:

```
public int Eval(string s)
{
   throw new Exception();
}
```

(Note: you will need to add *using System;* for this to compile.)

I run the tests again and – I get my first green! The specification worked and the *system under test* behaves as specified. Yes, it is a trivial specification but bear with me, we're going places.

Let me write the second unit test now: a one-digit number should be evaluated to its integer value:

```
[TestMethod]
public void OneDigitNumberIsEvaluatedToItsIntegerValue()
{
   var sut = new Evaluator();

   var result = sut.Eval("7");

   Assert.AreEqual(7, result);
}
```

The test fails incorrectly – it doesn't return the wrong result, it throws an exception. Returning 0 would fix that problem, but it would break the previous unit test. That means I need to add logic to the Eval method:

```
public int Eval(string s)
{
   if (string.IsNullOrEmpty(s))
      throw new Exception();

   return 0;
}
```

Now the second test fails correctly: "Assert.AreEqual failed. Expected:<7>. Actual:<0>." This is important – if the test fails for a different reason than expected it might not test what I actually wanted, which means I'm not as protected as I should be.

I've reached an important moment: one of the TDD principles is "do the simplest thing that could possibly work". The simplest thing, taken to extremes, is to simply return 7 from the Eval method, and there is a school of thought that would have us do exactly that. It is not as absurd as it sounds at first, so I'm going to show you what happens:

```
public int Eval(string s)
{
   if (string.IsNullOrEmpty(s))
     throw new Exception();

   return 7;
}
```

The two unit tests pass now. I realize there's a problem and I expose it through another test:

```
[TestMethod]
public void
OneDigitNumberIsEvaluatedToItsIntegerValue_SecondAttempt()
{
   var sut = new Evaluator();

   var result = sut.Eval("5");

   Assert.AreEqual(5, result);
}
```

The test fails correctly ("Assert.AreEqual failed. Expected:<5>. Actual:<7>.") so I need to fix the issue. What is the simplest thing that could possibly work now? It's definitely not "return 5;" and testing for 5 or 7 is more complex than just converting the string to a number:

```
public int Eval(string s)
{
   if (string.IsNullOrEmpty(s))
     throw new Exception();

   return Convert.ToInt32(s);
}
```

All our unit tests pass; as you can see, "do the simplest thing that could possibly work" was not as big of a problem as I initially feared. I can also see, by looking at the Eval method, that I'm actually supporting multiple-digit numbers too; I'll write a test to confirm that:

```
[TestMethod]
public void MultipleDigitNumberIsEvaluatedToItsIntegerValue()
{
    var sut = new Evaluator();

    var result = sut.Eval("324");

    Assert.AreEqual(324, result);
}
```

Indeed, this passes, and having a test here ensures that I don't change something that will break it.

Time for a short recap: I am going through very quick *write test – write code – make test pass* cycles, also known as red-green. This helps me in two ways: I get constant positive feedback from seeing that my code is working (which is, in my opinion, one of the greatest feelings in the world) and, whenever I need to stop for some reason, I am confident that I can get back "in the saddle" quickly, by re-reading the last tests I wrote.

> *Note: I have observed one problem while writing this book: the drawback of having a great "it works" feeling is that it also provides a natural time-out point. If you tend to procrastinate, the moment all tests pass is great for checking mail, calling someone, reading the news... anything but working. This does not normally happen when you're busy coding in the usual way, in my experience, because feedback occurs less*

> *often; it takes more discipline to keep working when doing TDD. A partner could probably help here, but I've never tried pair programming myself.*

There is also an important last step in the cycle, one that doesn't occur all the time: refactoring. The production code is quite simple so there's no need for it; however, the tests have a lot of duplication in them. Let's get rid of that: their purpose is to pass a string to the Eval method and compare it to the expected value. I'll write a helper method for it:

```
private static void CheckEvaluation(string s, int expected)
{
  var sut = new Evaluator();

  var result = sut.Eval(s);

  Assert.AreEqual(expected, result);
}
```

I test it first by changing a single test and re-running it:

```
[TestMethod]
public void MultipleDigitNumberIsEvaluatedToItsIntegerValue()
{
  CheckEvaluation("324", 324);
}
```

It appears to work, so here's the complete class, rewritten to use the new helper method:

```
[TestClass]
public class EvaluatorTests
{
  [TestMethod]
  [ExpectedException(typeof (Exception))]
  public void NullOrEmptyStringThrowsException()
  {
    var sut = new Evaluator();

    sut.Eval("");
  }
```

```
[TestMethod]
public void OneDigitNumberIsEvaluatedToItsIntegerValue()
{
   CheckEvaluation("7", 7);
}

[TestMethod]
public void
OneDigitNumberIsEvaluatedToItsIntegerValue_SecondAttempt()
{
   CheckEvaluation("5", 5);
}

[TestMethod]
public void MultipleDigitNumberIsEvaluatedToItsIntegerValue()
{
   CheckEvaluation("324", 324);
}

//

private static void CheckEvaluation(string s, int expected)
{
   var sut = new Evaluator();

   var result = sut.Eval(s);

   Assert.AreEqual(expected, result);
}
}
```

I did not change the first method because I didn't want to suggest the wrong idea to someone reading the tests; the Eval call is not supposed to return something meaningful in that case.

All the unit tests are still working and the duplication has been removed. This is a good start.

## 2.2. Addition

Time to attack the first acceptance test: adding two numbers. I start, as expected, by writing a unit test. I know that I have an acceptance test for it, but that's not the same thing. Acceptance tests are end-to-end tests; they test the whole system. Unit tests are for a single class. (I realize that right now the distinction is meaningless, but we're not going to have a single class forever.)

In any case, here's the first test:

```
[TestMethod]
public void AddingTwoNumbers()
{
   CheckEvaluation("1+2", 3);
}
```

It fails, of course, with the error "System.FormatException: Input string was not in a correct format." That is not a good reason to fail, so I need to do something about it. (A good reason to fail is an incorrect result.)

I can see two methods of fixing that, both quite simple: one would be to split the string at the '+' sign, and evaluate the first (or only) part being returned; the other would be to read the string until I encounter a non-digit character and evaluate the part before that index. The first algorithm appears to be simpler, so I'll go with that:

```
public int Eval(string s)
{
  if (string.IsNullOrEmpty(s))
    throw new Exception();

  var parts = s.Split('+');
  return Convert.ToInt32(parts[0]);
}
```

Now the test fails the "right" way: "Assert.AreEqual failed. Expected:<3>. Actual:<1>." Let's make it work:

```
public int Eval(string s)
{
  if (string.IsNullOrEmpty(s))
    throw new Exception();

  var parts = s.Split('+');
  return parts
    .Select(part => Convert.ToInt32(part))
    .Sum();
}
```

We're going to need an additional "`using System.Linq;`" to compile and then – 6 out of 7 tests are running! It seems that I have managed to get our first acceptance test to pass, which is a good milestone. In fact, looking back, I appear to be close to the "minimum feature list" goal in only a couple of hours of coding, which is not bad at all.

## 2.3. Subtraction

Let's tackle the next acceptance test, subtraction. I'll start by adding a new unit test:

```
[TestMethod]
public void SubtractingTwoNumbers()
{
  CheckEvaluation("88-20", 68);
}
```

It fails badly: "System.FormatException: Input string was not in a correct format." The quickest way of fixing that that I can think of is to try addition first, then subtraction, then evaluating a single number; that will ensure that the previous tests are still passing:

```
public int Eval(string s)
{
  if (string.IsNullOrEmpty(s))
```

```
        throw new Exception();

    string[] parts;
    if (s.IndexOf('+') >= 0)
    {
       parts = s.Split('+');
       return Convert.ToInt32(parts[0]) +
Convert.ToInt32(parts[1]);
    }
    else if (s.IndexOf('-') >= 0)
    {
       parts = s.Split('-');
       return Convert.ToInt32(parts[0]) -
Convert.ToInt32(parts[1]);
    }
    else
       return Convert.ToInt32(s);
}
```

All the tests pass, which is good but not enough: I need to refactor the code, otherwise I'm going to have a mighty mess on my hands. (This is the most dangerous part when you're coding: you're "in the zone", getting results and you don't want to stop and clean up the code. Technical debt accumulates very fast and soon, you can't make any progress anymore. Take the time after each unit test passes to look over the code and ask yourself: is there a way to make the code or the tests simpler? It will pay off.)

## 2.4. Refactoring

It appears that I need a way of splitting a string in parts, with each part being either an operand (a number) or an operator (like '+' or '-'). Let's create a method for that... by starting with a test:

```
[TestMethod]
public void ParseReturnsAdditionElements()
{
   var sut = new Evaluator();
```

```
    var result = sut.Parse("1+2").ToList();

    Assert.AreEqual(3, result.Count);
    Assert.IsInstanceOfType(result[0], typeof (Operand));
    Assert.IsInstanceOfType(result[1], typeof (Operator));
    Assert.IsInstanceOfType(result[2], typeof (Operand));
}
```

(Add "`using System.Linq;`" for the .ToList() extension method. I'm not going to keep mentioning this... either Visual Studio itself or the Resharper add-on, if you're using it, can tell you what `using`s you need to make the code compile.)

The test doesn't compile; I need to fix that, by creating the Operand and Operator classes and adding a public Parse method to the Evaluator class. Because the Parse method is supposed to return a List, I need for both Operand and Operator to inherit from the same class; let's call it Element. Right now, these three classes – Element, Operand and Operator – have no logic (and in fact no content), so I don't yet need any tests for them:

```
public abstract class Element
{
}

public class Operand : Element
{
}

public class Operator : Element
{
}
```

I start with an empty implementation for the Parse method; it shouldn't return null (that would fail with an exception) but instead return an empty list:

```
public IEnumerable<Element> Parse(string s)
{
    return new List<Element>();
```

}
```

This fails with "Assert.AreEqual failed. Expected:<3>. Actual:<0>." So far, so good.

## 2.5. Parsing

How do I make the test pass? I could use a finite state machine here, but I am not trying to find the best algorithm for evaluating an expression; I am trying to show the TDD process, so let's keep things simple. I am going to read characters and keep track of the current state:

```
public IEnumerable<Element> Parse(string s)
{
  var operand = "";
  foreach (var currentChar in s)
  {
    if (char.IsDigit(currentChar))
      operand += currentChar;
    else
    {
      yield return new Operand(operand);
      operand = "";

      yield return new Operator(currentChar);
    }
  }

  if (operand != "")
    yield return new Operand(operand);
}
```

In order to compile, I need to add constructors to the Operand and Operator classes:

```
public class Operand : Element
{
  public Operand(string s)
  {
    //
  }
}
```
```

```
public class Operator : Element
{
  public Operator(char c)
  {
    //
  }
}
```

The tests pass. I can now refactor the Eval method to use the new classes:

```
public int Eval(string s)
{
  if (string.IsNullOrEmpty(s))
    throw new Exception();

  var elements = Parse(s).ToList();

  if (elements[1].Value == "+")
    return Convert.ToInt32(elements[0].Value) + Convert.ToInt32(elements[2].Value);
  if (elements[1].Value == "-")
    return Convert.ToInt32(elements[0].Value) - Convert.ToInt32(elements[2].Value);

  return Convert.ToInt32(s);
}
```

I need a Value property on both the operands and the operators; this tells me what to put in the constructors. I'll make sure I got those covered by tests too:

```
[TestClass]
public class OperandTests
{
  [TestMethod]
  public void ConstructorSetsValuePropertyCorrectly()
  {
    var sut = new Operand("123");

    Assert.AreEqual("123", sut.Value);
  }
}
```

```
[TestClass]
public class OperatorTests
{
  [TestMethod]
  public void ConstructorSetsValuePropertyCorrectly()
  {
    var sut = new Operator('+');

    Assert.AreEqual("+", sut.Value);
  }
}
```

The classes get changed to:

```
public abstract class Element
{
  public string Value { get; protected set; }
}

public class Operand : Element
{
  public Operand(string s)
  {
    Value = s;
  }
}

public class Operator : Element
{
  public Operator(char c)
  {
    Value = c.ToString();
  }
}
```

The tests compile, but now I have three failing tests. A quick check tells me that I'm accessing an inexistent index. That is easily fixed:

```
public int Eval(string s)
{
  if (string.IsNullOrEmpty(s))
    throw new Exception();

  var elements = Parse(s).ToList();
```

```
    if (elements.Count == 3)
    {
        if (elements[1].Value == "+")
            return Convert.ToInt32(elements[0].Value) +
Convert.ToInt32(elements[2].Value);
        if (elements[1].Value == "-")
            return Convert.ToInt32(elements[0].Value) -
Convert.ToInt32(elements[2].Value);
    }

    return Convert.ToInt32(s);
}
```

All tests pass now. I'm still far from being done with the refactoring, though – there is still a lot of duplication in the code. Let's take care of it.

### 2.6. *Extracting a new class*

A class should only have one responsibility. The Evaluator class has three:

- It parses the expression
- It identifies the operators
- Finally, it executes the correct calculation depending on the operator

Let's start by extracting the Parse method into its own class. I'll create a new test class and move the `ParseReturnsAdditionElements()` method there:

```
[TestClass]
public class ParserTests
{
    [TestMethod]
    public void ParseReturnsAdditionElements()
    {
        var sut = new Parser();

        var result = sut.Parse("1+2").ToList();
```

```
    Assert.AreEqual(3, result.Count);
    Assert.IsInstanceOfType(result[0], typeof (Operand));
    Assert.IsInstanceOfType(result[1], typeof (Operator));
    Assert.IsInstanceOfType(result[2], typeof (Operand));
  }
}
```

I need a new Parser class:

```
public class Parser
{
  public IEnumerable<Element> Parse(string s)
  {
    var operand = "";
    foreach (var currentChar in s)
    {
      if (char.IsDigit(currentChar))
        operand += currentChar;
      else
      {
        yield return new Operand(operand);
        operand = "";

        yield return new Operator(currentChar);
      }
    }

    if (operand != "")
      yield return new Operand(operand);
  }
}
```

The Evaluator class will change accordingly:

```
public class Evaluator
{
  public int Eval(string s)
  {
    if (string.IsNullOrEmpty(s))
      throw new Exception();

    var parser = new Parser();
    var elements = parser.Parse(s).ToList();

    if (elements.Count == 3)
```

```
    {
       if (elements[1].Value == "+")
          return Convert.ToInt32(elements[0].Value) + Convert.ToInt32(elements[2].Value);
       if (elements[1].Value == "-")
          return Convert.ToInt32(elements[0].Value) - Convert.ToInt32(elements[2].Value);
    }

    return Convert.ToInt32(s);
  }
}
```

All the tests are still passing.

### 2.7. Operators

The class responsible for knowing how to compute an operation should, logically, be the operator itself. Let's add a test for that:

```
[TestMethod]
public void AdditionOperatorComputesCorrectValue()
{
   var sut = new Operator('+');

   var result = sut.Compute(10, 20);

   Assert.AreEqual(30, result);
}
```

Making the test compile is simple:

```
public int Compute(int left, int right)
{
   return 0;
}
```

The test fails; making it pass is also simple:

```
public int Compute(int left, int right)
{
   return left + right;
}
```

I need a new test for subtraction:

```
[TestMethod]
public void SubtractionOperatorComputesCorrectValue()
{
  var sut = new Operator('-');

  var result = sut.Compute(20, 10);

  Assert.AreEqual(10, result);
}
```

This test fails too; making it work yields this:

```
public int Compute(int left, int right)
{
  switch (Value)
  {
    case "+":
      return left + right;
    default:
      return left - right;
  }
}
```

Observation: I did not add a case for "-" because we'd have been left with an undefined behavior for an the default case. Let's decide that an unknown operator will throw an exception and write a test for that:

```
[TestMethod]
[ExpectedException(typeof (Exception))]
public void UnknownOperatorThrowsOnCompute()
{
  var sut = new Operator('x');

  sut.Compute(0, 0);
}
```

The test fails, because the Compute method does not throw an exception; let's make it pass:

```
public int Compute(int left, int right)
{
```

```
    switch (Value)
    {
      case "+":
        return left + right;
      case "-":
        return left - right;
      default:
        throw new Exception("Unknown operator " + Value);
    }
  }
```

All tests pass again. I can now refactor the Eval method:

```
  public int Eval(string s)
  {
    if (string.IsNullOrEmpty(s))
      throw new Exception();

    var parser = new Parser();
    var elements = parser.Parse(s).ToList();

    if (elements.Count == 3)
    {
      var op = elements[1] as Operator;
      return op.Compute(Convert.ToInt32(elements[0].Value),
Convert.ToInt32(elements[2].Value));
    }

    return Convert.ToInt32(s);
  }
```

I have a much better design than before, but there's still room for improvement. I start by observing that the only outside user of the Value property of the Operator class is the test. I can change it to a private field inside the class and move the property to the Operand class:

```
  public class Operator : Element
  {
    public Operator(char c)
    {
      value = c;
    }

    public int Compute(int left, int right)
```

## TDD by example – Evaluating an expression

```
    {
      switch (value)
      {
        case '+':
          return left + right;
        case '-':
          return left - right;
        default:
          throw new Exception("Unknown operator " + value);
      }
    }
    //
    private readonly char value;
  }
  public class Operand : Element
  {
    public string Value { get; private set; }

    public Operand(string s)
    {
      Value = s;
    }
  }
```

I remove the first test from the OperatorTests class (the one using the now-deleted property Value) and change the Eval function to compile:

```
    public int Eval(string s)
    {
      if (string.IsNullOrEmpty(s))
        throw new Exception();

      var parser = new Parser();
      var elements = parser.Parse(s).ToList();

      if (elements.Count == 3)
      {
        var op = elements[1] as Operator;
        var left = elements[0] as Operand;
        var right = elements[2] as Operand;
        return op.Compute(Convert.ToInt32(left.Value),
Convert.ToInt32(right.Value));
```

```
    }

    return Convert.ToInt32(s);
}
```

Since the Value property only exists on operands now, I can change its type to int:

```
public class Operand : Element
{
  public int Value { get; private set; }

  public Operand(string s)
  {
    Value = Convert.ToInt32(s);
  }
}
```

The test in the OperandTests class needs to change too:

```
[TestMethod]
public void ConstructorSetsValuePropertyCorrectly()
{
   var sut = new Operand("123");

   Assert.AreEqual(123, sut.Value);
}
```

I'll change the Eval method:

```
public int Eval(string s)
{
  if (string.IsNullOrEmpty(s))
    throw new Exception();

  var parser = new Parser();
  var elements = parser.Parse(s).ToList();

  if (elements.Count == 3)
  {
    var left = elements[0] as Operand;
    var op = elements[1] as Operator;
    var right = elements[2] as Operand;

    return op.Compute(left.Value, right.Value);
  }
```

```
    return Convert.ToInt32(s);
  }
```

Hmm... all tests pass, but something's still not right: the operators should work on operands, not on ints. Let's fix that by altering the operator tests:

```
[TestClass]
public class OperatorTests
{
  [TestMethod]
  public void AdditionOperatorComputesCorrectValue()
  {
    var sut = new Operator('+');

    var result = sut.Compute(new Operand("10"), new Operand("20"));

    Assert.AreEqual(30, result);
  }

  [TestMethod]
  public void SubtractionOperatorComputesCorrectValue()
  {
    var sut = new Operator('-');

    var result = sut.Compute(new Operand("20"), new Operand("10"));

    Assert.AreEqual(10, result);
  }

  [TestMethod]
  [ExpectedException(typeof (Exception))]
  public void UnknownOperatorThrowsOnCompute()
  {
    var sut = new Operator('x');

    sut.Compute(new Operand("0"), new Operand("0"));
  }
}
```

The Compute method of the Operator class needs to change:

```
public int Compute(Operand left, Operand right)
{
  switch (value)
  {
    case '+':
      return left.Value + right.Value;
    case '-':
      return left.Value - right.Value;
    default:
      throw new Exception("Unknown operator " + value);
  }
}
```

Finally (for real this time!) I have a clean version of the Eval method:

```
public int Eval(string s)
{
  if (string.IsNullOrEmpty(s))
    throw new Exception();

  var parser = new Parser();
  var elements = parser.Parse(s).ToList();

  if (elements.Count == 3)
  {
    var left = elements[0] as Operand;
    var op = elements[1] as Operator;
    var right = elements[2] as Operand;

    return op.Compute(left, right);
  }

  return Convert.ToInt32(s);
}
```

I have reached the minimum feature set as indicated by the acceptance tests; furthermore, the design is quite clean – anybody who tries to understand the code should have no problem doing that.

There's still a problem with the Operator class though – that switch statement looks really ugly. I need to replace it. The correct, object-oriented way of replacing a switch statement is creating a class hierarchy and moving that switch statement to a factory object (there are ways to remove the switch altogether, but I don't know if I need to go that deep right now). Let's see what the tests for this factory object look like:

```
[TestClass]
public class OperatorFactoryTests
{
  [TestMethod]
  public void PlusSignReturnsAddOperator()
  {
    var sut = new OperatorFactory();

    var result = sut.Create('+');

    Assert.IsInstanceOfType(result, typeof (AddOperator));
  }
}
```

I'll make the test compile and fail correctly:

```
public class OperatorFactory
{
  public Operator Create(char op)
  {
    return null;
  }
}

public class AddOperator : Operator
{
  public AddOperator() : base('+')
  {
  }
}
```

The test fails because we're not returning the correct instance; let's fix that:

```
public Operator Create(char op)
{
  return new AddOperator();
}
```

All tests pass now. I need to add the test for the subtract operator too:

```
[TestMethod]
public void MinusSignReturnsSubOperator()
{
   var sut = new OperatorFactory();

   var result = sut.Create('-');

   Assert.IsInstanceOfType(result, typeof(SubOperator));
}
```

Creating the SubOperator class makes the test compile and fail correctly:

```
public class SubOperator : Operator
{
  public SubOperator() : base('-')
  {
  }
}
```

The change to make the test pass is simple:

```
public Operator Create(char op)
{
    return op == '+' ? (Operator) new AddOperator() : new SubOperator();
}
```

I don't like the way that looks though. I've decided that an unknown operator will throw an exception:

```
[TestMethod]
[ExpectedException(typeof (Exception))]
public void UnknownSignThrowsException()
{
   var sut = new OperatorFactory();

   sut.Create('x');
}
```

This allows me to return to the switch statement in the Create method:

```
public Operator Create(char op)
{
  switch (op)
  {
    case '+':
      return new AddOperator();
    case '-':
      return new SubOperator();
    default:
      throw new Exception();
  }
}
```

All the tests pass. I can now refactor the Parse method in the Parser class:

```
public IEnumerable<Element> Parse(string s)
{
  var operatorFactory = new OperatorFactory();

  var operand = "";
  foreach (var currentChar in s)
  {
    if (char.IsDigit(currentChar))
      operand += currentChar;
    else
    {
      yield return new Operand(operand);
      operand = "";

      yield return operatorFactory.Create(currentChar);
    }
  }

  if (operand != "")
    yield return new Operand(operand);
}
```

I check that nothing got broken by rerunning the tests; they all pass. I can now remove the switch statement from the operator class and move the actual computation to the leaf classes. Since I'm adding logic to the AddOperator and SubOperator classes, I need to add tests too (I'm basically moving the ones from the OperatorTests class):

```
[TestClass]
public class AddOperatorTests
{
  [TestMethod]
  public void AddOperatorComputesCorrectValue()
  {
    var sut = new AddOperator();

    var result = sut.Compute(new Operand("10"), new Operand("20"));

    Assert.AreEqual(30, result);
  }
}
```

This test is still passing – that's because the Operator.Compute method hasn't been changed yet. I'm getting there.

```
[TestClass]
public class SubOperatorTests
{
  [TestMethod]
  public void SubtractionOperatorComputesCorrectValue()
  {
    var sut = new SubOperator();

    var result = sut.Compute(new Operand("20"), new Operand("10"));

    Assert.AreEqual(10, result);
  }
}
```

I can now move the logic out from the Operator class into the leaf classes; by doing that, I discover that I don't need the value field at all:

```
public abstract class Operator : Element
{
  public abstract int Compute(Operand left, Operand right);
```

```
}
public class AddOperator : Operator
{
  public override int Compute(Operand left, Operand right)
  {
    return left.Value + right.Value;
  }
}
public class SubOperator : Operator
{
  public override int Compute(Operand left, Operand right)
  {
    return left.Value - right.Value;
  }
}
```

The OperatorTests class is useless now, so I remove it. The tests compile and pass.

I have reached a good point. The Evaluator class can be used for adding or subtracting two integers and the design of the classes is clean. The classes are small and mostly well-named. Also importantly, I'm quite sure everything works correctly.

What's next?

## Chapter 3. More operations

Adding more operations should be quite simple now. I'll start with new acceptance tests – I've decided that the next "release" of my code will handle (integer) multiplication and division too:

```
[TestMethod]
public void CanMultiplyTwoIntegerNumbers()
{
  var sut = new Evaluator();

  var result = sut.Eval("12*30");

  Assert.AreEqual(360, result);
}

[TestMethod]
public void CanDivideTwoIntegerNumbers()
{
  var sut = new Evaluator();

  var result = sut.Eval("30/5");

  Assert.AreEqual(6, result);
}
```

The tests fail with an obscure message: "System.Exception: Exception of type 'System.Exception' was thrown." Since that looks pretty bad, let's fix it first; the exception is thrown in the OperatorFactory.Create method:

```
public Operator Create(char op)
{
  switch (op)
  {
    case '+':
      return new AddOperator();
    case '-':
      return new SubOperator();
    default:
      throw new Exception(string.Format("Unknown operator [{0}]", op));
  }
```

        }

The error message is now a much better "System.Exception: Unknown operator [/]". Good.

There's also the problem of repetition in the acceptance tests. I'll just copy the same method I'm using in the EvaluatorTests class; if I need it in a third place I'll extract it in a helper class:

> *Note: I have a rule-of-thumb to decide when to remove duplication: I (generally) only do it if I've seen the same thing three times. I can't really justify it; use it or not as you see fit.*[4]

```
[TestClass]
public class AcceptanceTests
{
   [TestMethod]
   public void CanAddTwoIntegerNumbers()
   {
      CheckEvaluation("10+25", 35);
   }

   [TestMethod]
   public void CanSubtractTwoIntegerNumbers()
   {
      CheckEvaluation("300-5", 295);
   }

   [TestMethod]
   public void CanMultiplyTwoIntegerNumbers()
   {
      CheckEvaluation("12*30", 360);
   }

   [TestMethod]
   public void CanDivideTwoIntegerNumbers()
   {
      CheckEvaluation("30/5", 6);
   }
```

---

[4] I found the source of this rule at http://c2.com/cgi/wiki?ThreeStrikesAndYouRefactor

```
    //
    private static void CheckEvaluation(string s, int expected)
    {
       var sut = new Evaluator();
       var result = sut.Eval(s);
       Assert.AreEqual(expected, result);
    }
}
```

All the tests except for the last two pass, so I haven't broken anything.

I need to add a unit test (again, it helps to think of it as an *executable specification*) to the EvaluatorTests class:

```
[TestMethod]
public void MultiplyingTwoNumbers()
{
   CheckEvaluation("12*3", 36);
}
```

However, there is nothing I can do inside the Evaluator class itself to fix the failed test. I am, to be honest, unsure if I actually need this test here, especially since it pretty much duplicates the acceptance test. I might come back later and delete it.

In the meantime, where do I need to change the code to make the test pass? I need a new operator, so I start with a test there:

```
[TestClass]
public class MulOperatorTests
{
   [TestMethod]
   public void MulOperatorComputesCorrectValue()
   {
      var sut = new MulOperator();
```

```
        var result = sut.Compute(new Operand("10"), new
Operand("25"));

        Assert.AreEqual(250, result);
    }
}
```

Hmm... I'm starting to dislike the idea of passing a string to the Operand constructor... I'll have to come back to that. Until then, though, I need to create the MulOperator class:

```
public class MulOperator : Operator
{
  public override int Compute(Operand left, Operand right)
  {
    return 0;
  }
}
```

Everything compiles and the test fails with "Assert.AreEqual failed. Expected:<250>. Actual:<0>." Good. Easy to fix:

```
public override int Compute(Operand left, Operand right)
{
  return left.Value * right.Value;
}
```

The acceptance tests are still failing, though, because the operator "*" is not known. Let's first specify what is supposed to happen, by adding a test to the OperatorFactoryTests class:

```
[TestMethod]
public void AsteriskSignReturnsMulOperator()
{
  var sut = new OperatorFactory();

  var result = sut.Create('*');

  Assert.IsInstanceOfType(result, typeof (MulOperator));
}
```

The test fails; I can fix that:

```
    public Operator Create(char op)
    {
      switch (op)
      {
        case '+':
          return new AddOperator();
        case '-':
          return new SubOperator();
        case '*':
          return new MulOperator();
        default:
          throw new Exception(string.Format("Unknown operator [{0}]", op));
      }
    }
```

Success – all the tests pass, except for the acceptance test for division. Good.

### 3.1. Refactoring

Let's refactor the OperatorFactoryTests class, there's too much repetition in there. First of all, I want to extract the creation of the *system under test* into a private field and create it automatically before each test. I know there are people against using the [TestInitialize] methods or their equivalents, but I think this is a legitimate use:

```
    private OperatorFactory sut;

    [TestInitialize]
    public void SetUp()
    {
       sut = new OperatorFactory();
    }
```

I then remove the initialization of the sut variable from each test and rerun them; they all still pass (except for the acceptance test for division), so I haven't broken anything.

## TDD by example – Evaluating an expression

One more change – move the Create call and the assertion to a common method and I'm done:

```
[TestClass]
public class OperatorFactoryTests
{
  private OperatorFactory sut;

  [TestInitialize]
  public void SetUp()
  {
    sut = new OperatorFactory();
  }

  [TestMethod]
  public void PlusSignReturnsAddOperator()
  {
    Check('+', typeof (AddOperator));
  }

  [TestMethod]
  public void MinusSignReturnsSubOperator()
  {
    Check('-', typeof (SubOperator));
  }

  [TestMethod]
  [ExpectedException(typeof (Exception))]
  public void UnknownSignThrowsException()
  {
    sut.Create('x');
  }

  [TestMethod]
  public void AsteriskSignReturnsMulOperator()
  {
    Check('*', typeof (MulOperator));
  }

  //

  private void Check(char op, Type type)
  {
    var result = sut.Create(op);

    Assert.IsInstanceOfType(result, type);
```

        }
    }

Nothing got broken, and the tests are clearer now – there's less ceremony and more substance. Good.

## 3.2. Division

Making the final acceptance test pass should be a breeze. I'll add the unit test to the EvaluatorTests class, if only because I haven't decided whether it's needed or not:

```
[TestMethod]
public void DividingTwoNumbers()
{
    CheckEvaluation("12/3", 4);
}
```

One important thing to note is that I'm going to be careful that my divisions only return integers. I don't want to handle floating point numbers yet.

I add the new unit test class:

```
[TestClass]
public class DivOperatorTests
{
    [TestMethod]
    public void DivOperatorComputesCorrectValue()
    {
        var sut = new DivOperator();

        var result = sut.Compute(new Operand("20"), new Operand("10"));

        Assert.AreEqual(2, result);
    }
}
```

and make it compile by writing the DivOperator class:

```
public class DivOperator : Operator
```

```
{
  public override int Compute(Operand left, Operand right)
  {
    return 0;
  }
}
```

I know that, by this time, you're asking yourself why I don't just go straight to the correct implementation. I recommend against it, at least until you've been doing this for a while; making the test fail first is a good habit to get into. You want to make sure the tests are failing because the method being tested is incorrect, not because of some other unrelated reason.

Now that I confirmed that the test is failing ("Assert.AreEqual failed. Expected:<2>. Actual:<0>."), I can make it work:

```
public override int Compute(Operand left, Operand right)
{
  return left.Value / right.Value;
}
```

All that remains is returning the correct instance for the "/" operator:

```
[TestMethod]
public void SlashSignReturnsDivOperator()
{
  Check('/', typeof (DivOperator));
}
```

Once I change the OperatorFactory.Create method, all tests pass:

```
public Operator Create(char op)
{
  switch (op)
  {
    case '+':
      return new AddOperator();
```

```
      case '-':
        return new SubOperator();
      case '*':
        return new MulOperator();
      case '/':
        return new DivOperator();
      default:
        throw new Exception(string.Format("Unknown operator [{0}]", op));
    }
  }
```

I have two more acceptance tests working; two more operations that the code can handle.

### 3.3. Refactoring

As I said earlier, I don't like the idea of Operand's constructor taking a string. Transforming a string into a number is something the parser should do, not the Operand. Let's alter the Operand test:

```
[TestMethod]
public void ConstructorSetsValuePropertyCorrectly()
{
   var sut = new Operand(123);

   Assert.AreEqual(123, sut.Value);
}
```

This means changing the constructor:

```
public Operand(int value)
{
   Value = value;
}
```

and the parser (right now the Parse method doesn't compile). Unfortunately, there's no test I can change here; I don't like that. There should be no code changes without a test change.

Looking at the Parse method, I see the Operand instances are new'd directly; it's a good idea in most cases not to do that, but to pass a factory instead. (The reason you should not new an object directly in the code is because it violates the Dependency Inversion Principle I've mentioned before.) Furthermore, the OperatorFactory is also new'd inside the method, which is bordering on absurd.

We'll take it easy with the changes; first, I'll make it compile so I know that nothing was broken:

```
public IEnumerable<Element> Parse(string s)
{
  var operatorFactory = new OperatorFactory();

  var operand = "";
  foreach (var currentChar in s)
  {
    if (char.IsDigit(currentChar))
      operand += currentChar;
    else
    {
      yield return new Operand(Convert.ToInt32(operand));
      operand = "";

      yield return operatorFactory.Create(currentChar);
    }
  }

  if (operand != "")
    yield return new Operand(Convert.ToInt32(operand));
}
```

I compile it and... oops, the individual operator tests are also failing, so I need to change them too:

```
[TestMethod]
public void AddOperatorComputesCorrectValue()
{
  var sut = new AddOperator();

  var result = sut.Compute(new Operand(10), new Operand(20));
```

```
    Assert.AreEqual(30, result);
}

[TestMethod]
public void SubtractionOperatorComputesCorrectValue()
{
    var sut = new SubOperator();

    var result = sut.Compute(new Operand(20), new Operand(10));

    Assert.AreEqual(10, result);
}

[TestMethod]
public void MulOperatorComputesCorrectValue()
{
    var sut = new MulOperator();

    var result = sut.Compute(new Operand(10), new Operand(25));

    Assert.AreEqual(250, result);
}

[TestMethod]
public void DivOperatorComputesCorrectValue()
{
    var sut = new DivOperator();

    var result = sut.Compute(new Operand(20), new Operand(10));

    Assert.AreEqual(2, result);
}
```

Ok, everything compiles and the tests pass. Good. Back to the Parse method; the operatorFactory should be injected into the constructor:

```
public class Parser
{
    public Parser(OperatorFactory operatorFactory)
    {
        this.operatorFactory = operatorFactory;
    }

    public IEnumerable<Element> Parse(string s)
```

```
{
  var operand = "";
  foreach (var currentChar in s)
  {
    if (char.IsDigit(currentChar))
      operand += currentChar;
    else
    {
      yield return new Operand(Convert.ToInt32(operand));
      operand = "";

      yield return operatorFactory.Create(currentChar);
    }
  }

  if (operand != "")
    yield return new Operand(Convert.ToInt32(operand));
}
//

private readonly OperatorFactory operatorFactory;
}
```

The ParserTests class doesn't compile, let's fix that:

```
public void ParseReturnsAdditionElements()
{
  var sut = new Parser(new OperatorFactory());

  var result = sut.Parse("1+2").ToList();

  Assert.AreEqual(3, result.Count);
  Assert.IsInstanceOfType(result[0], typeof (Operand));
  Assert.IsInstanceOfType(result[1], typeof (Operator));
  Assert.IsInstanceOfType(result[2], typeof (Operand));
}
```

Unfortunately, neither does the Evaluator.Eval method... which creates a Parser instance instead of having one injected. I am pretty upset that I missed this. Small steps, though, so we're making everything compile first:

```
public int Eval(string s)
{
```

```
    if (string.IsNullOrEmpty(s))
      throw new Exception();

    var parser = new Parser(new OperatorFactory());
    var elements = parser.Parse(s).ToList();

    if (elements.Count == 3)
    {
      var left = elements[0] as Operand;
      var op = elements[1] as Operator;
      var right = elements[2] as Operand;

      return op.Compute(left, right);
    }

    return Convert.ToInt32(s);
}
```

Good. The Parser class still receives an instance of an actual class but, since I am not sure about the advantage of extracting an interface in this case I decide to leave it as it is for now.

I still need to extract the new-ing of the Operand though; that means an OperandFactory class, which means an OperandFactoryTests unit test:

```
[TestClass]
public class OperandFactoryTests
{
  [TestMethod]
  public void CreateReturnsOperand()
  {
    var sut = new OperandFactory();

    var result = sut.Create(5);

    Assert.IsInstanceOfType(result, typeof (Operand));
  }
}
```

Making it compile is simple:

```
public class OperandFactory
{
```

```
    public Operand Create(int value)
    {
      return null;
    }
}
```

The test fails because I'm not returning the correct type, so let's do the simplest thing that can make it pass:

```
public class OperandFactory
{
  public Operand Create(int value)
  {
    return new Operand(0);
  }
}
```

The test passes; the fact that I haven't used the value tells me I need another test:

```
[TestMethod]
public void CreateReturnsOperandWithCorrectValue()
{
  var sut = new OperandFactory();

  var result = sut.Create(5);

  Assert.AreEqual(5, result.Value);
}
```

The test fails correctly (that is, because the Value property is not 5), so I make it pass:

```
public Operand Create(int value)
{
  return new Operand(value);
}
```

All is good.

Back to the Parse method; the Parser will need an OperandFactory argument to its constructor, so I modify the test:

```
[TestMethod]
public void ParseReturnsAdditionElements()
{
   var sut = new Parser(new OperatorFactory(), new
OperandFactory());

   var result = sut.Parse("1+2").ToList();

   Assert.AreEqual(3, result.Count);
   Assert.IsInstanceOfType(result[0], typeof (Operand));
   Assert.IsInstanceOfType(result[1], typeof (Operator));
   Assert.IsInstanceOfType(result[2], typeof (Operand));
}
```

The simplest way to make it compile is to just accept the additional argument and not do anything with it:

```
public Parser(OperatorFactory operatorFactory, OperandFactory
operandFactory)
{
   this.operatorFactory = operatorFactory;
}
```

The Evaluator.Eval method also needs to be changed:

```
public int Eval(string s)
{
  if (string.IsNullOrEmpty(s))
    throw new Exception();

  var parser = new Parser(new OperatorFactory(), new
OperandFactory());
  var elements = parser.Parse(s).ToList();

  if (elements.Count == 3)
  {
    var left = elements[0] as Operand;
    var op = elements[1] as Operator;
    var right = elements[2] as Operand;

    return op.Compute(left, right);
  }

  return Convert.ToInt32(s);
}
```

All tests pass... which is bad, because I'm not doing anything with the operandFactory argument. Oops.

## 3.4. Mocking

Now... the fastest way of fixing this is to go ahead and make the changes I know I should make – add a private operandFactory field, assign it in the constructor and use it in the Parse method. The **correct** way is to write a test exposing the problem. As before, I am going to show you the correct way; you can skip ahead to 3.5 if you want, but I don't recommend it if you're new to all this TDD stuff (and if you're not, you're probably bored to tears already).

Ok. Back to serious business. I need to verify that the Create method of the operandFactory object has actually been called. That means I need a mocking framework... and, since most mocking frameworks only work with interfaces, it means I need to extract an interface from the OperandFactory class.

Let's start with the mocking framework; I prefer the Moq framework myself, but most of the others should behave similarly. Right-click the References folder in the Math.ExpressionEvaluator.Tests project and choose the "Manage NuGet Packages" command; search for "Moq" in the Online category, click Install in the first item and then close the window.

I now need to extract an interface from the OperandFactory class; I'll name it IOperandFactory, even though I am very much against the idea of naming interfaces with an "I", because I just can't come up with a name for it. (In fact, I think OperandFactory should be the interface, but I can't come up with a name for the implementing class, so that doesn't help.)

I'll just use IOperandFactory until I can come up with something better:

```
public interface IOperandFactory
{
  Operand Create(int value);
}

public class OperandFactory : IOperandFactory
{
  public Operand Create(int value)
  {
    return new Operand(value);
  }
}
```

The Parser class should depend on the interface:

```
    public Parser(OperatorFactory operatorFactory, IOperandFactory operandFactory)
    {
        this.operatorFactory = operatorFactory;
    }
```

I can now write the test to verify that the IOperandFactory.Create method is being called:

```
    [TestMethod]
    public void ParseCallsOperandFactoryCreate()
    {
      var operandFactory = new Mock<IOperandFactory>();
      operandFactory
        .Setup(it => it.Create(It.IsAny<int>()))
        .Verifiable();

      var sut = new Parser(new OperatorFactory(), operandFactory.Object);

      sut.Parse("1").ToList();

      operandFactory.Verify();
    }
```

# TDD by example – Evaluating an expression

This will require some explaining. I started by creating the mock – a fake implementation of the IOperandFactory interface that I can use to (in this case) verify that a particular method is being called:

```
var operandFactory = new Mock<IOperandFactory>();
```

I tell the mock object which call I want to monitor and indicate that I don't care about the actual value being passed to it:

```
operandFactory
    .Setup(it => it.Create(It.IsAny<int>()))
    .Verifiable();
```

When I create the Parser object I can't give it the mock object directly (the mock object has all these additional methods, and it is not actually an IOperandFactory); instead, I use the Object property, which implements the desired interface:

```
var sut = new Parser(new OperatorFactory(), operandFactory.Object);
```

I now invoke the Parse method; the ToList() call is there to ensure that the method is actually being executed (an iterator method is not executed until you're actually starting to use the elements it returns):

```
sut.Parse("1").ToList();
```

Finally, I verify that the method I wanted to monitor was called:

```
operandFactory.Verify();
```

I run the tests and, of course, the verification fails with "Moq.MockVerificationException: The following setups were not matched: IOperandFactory it => it.Create(It.IsAny<Int32>())".

I can now fix the Parser class as I described earlier:

```
public class Parser
{
    public Parser(OperatorFactory operatorFactory, IOperandFactory operandFactory)
    {
        this.operatorFactory = operatorFactory;
        this.operandFactory = operandFactory;
    }

    public IEnumerable<Element> Parse(string s)
    {
        var operand = "";
        foreach (var currentChar in s)
        {
            if (char.IsDigit(currentChar))
                operand += currentChar;
            else
            {
                yield return operandFactory.Create(Convert.ToInt32(operand));
                operand = "";

                yield return operatorFactory.Create(currentChar);
            }
        }

        if (operand != "")
            yield return operandFactory.Create(Convert.ToInt32(operand));
    }

    //

    private readonly OperatorFactory operatorFactory;
    private readonly IOperandFactory operandFactory;
}
```

All tests pass – success!

## 3.5. More dependencies

I haven't forgotten about the hidden dependency in the Evaluator class. The Parser should be injected in the constructor, not created inside the method. The CheckEvaluation helper method and the first test in the EvaluatorTests class should be changed:

```
[TestMethod]
[ExpectedException(typeof (Exception))]
public void NullOrEmptyStringThrowsException()
{
    var parser = new Parser(new OperatorFactory(), new OperandFactory());
    var sut = new Evaluator(parser);

    sut.Eval("");
}

private static void CheckEvaluation(string s, int expected)
{
    var parser = new Parser(new OperatorFactory(), new OperandFactory());
    var sut = new Evaluator(parser);

    var result = sut.Eval(s);

    Assert.AreEqual(expected, result);
}
```

I'll change the Evaluator class to work correctly; I'm not going to go through the mocking stage again, even though I am afraid I might come to regret it:

```
public class Evaluator
{
  public Evaluator(Parser parser)
  {
    this.parser = parser;
  }

  public int Eval(string s)
  {
    if (string.IsNullOrEmpty(s))
      throw new Exception();

    var elements = parser.Parse(s).ToList();

    if (elements.Count == 3)
```

```
    {
      var left = elements[0] as Operand;
      var op = elements[1] as Operator;
      var right = elements[2] as Operand;

      return op.Compute(left, right);
    }

    return Convert.ToInt32(s);
  }

  //

  private readonly Parser parser;
}
```

The AcceptanceTests class complains about it, so *its* CheckEvaluation method needs changing too:

```
private static void CheckEvaluation(string s, int expected)
{
    var parser = new Parser(new OperatorFactory(), new OperandFactory());
    var sut = new Evaluator(parser);

    var result = sut.Eval(s);

    Assert.AreEqual(expected, result);
}
```

(As you can see, the duplication I haven't removed earlier is starting to become a problem. I want to finish this stage, though, so I continue to ignore it.)

All tests pass; I now have a cleaner design than I had at the start of this chapter, plus two new operations. Might not seem like a lot, but – if you followed along – this whole process should not have taken more than a few hours.

Next chapter we're going to attack multiple operations.

## Chapter 4. Multiple operations

Ok... until now we've only handled a single operation. Let's see how I can evaluate more than that, by adding an acceptance test:

```
[TestMethod]
public void MultipleOperations()
{
   CheckEvaluation("2+3*5-8/2", 13);
}
```

I don't yet want to handle operator precedence so I'll avoid that in the unit test (the EvaluatorTests class):

```
[TestMethod]
public void TwoOperations()
{
   CheckEvaluation("2*3-5", 1);
}
```

The test fails on the last line of the Evaluator.Eval method. Since it got there, I'm assuming that the parser did not return 3 elements... but I'll write a test to check that:

```
[TestMethod]
public void MultipleOperandAndOperatorsAreParsedCorrectly()
{
    var sut = new Parser(new OperatorFactory(), new OperandFactory());

    var result = sut.Parse("1+2*3-4").ToList();

    Assert.AreEqual(7, result.Count);
    Assert.IsInstanceOfType(result[0], typeof(Operand));
    Assert.IsInstanceOfType(result[1], typeof(Operator));
    Assert.IsInstanceOfType(result[2], typeof(Operand));
    Assert.IsInstanceOfType(result[3], typeof(Operator));
    Assert.IsInstanceOfType(result[4], typeof(Operand));
    Assert.IsInstanceOfType(result[5], typeof(Operator));
    Assert.IsInstanceOfType(result[6], typeof(Operand));
}
```

It passes; good.

Back to the Eval method: how to I handle the (normal) case with more than just 3 elements? The answer is rather obvious: I go through all the elements, from left to right, and replace the first (operand, operator, operand) tuple I encounter with the result of the operation; each time I do that, I restart the whole thing from the beginning (since I've changed the number of elements):

```
public class Evaluator
{
  public Evaluator(Parser parser)
  {
    this.parser = parser;
  }

  public int Eval(string s)
  {
    if (string.IsNullOrEmpty(s))
      throw new Exception();

    var elements = parser.Parse(s).ToList();

    while (elements.Count > 1)
    {
      var tupleIndex = FindOperation(elements);
      var newElement = Compute(elements[tupleIndex], elements[tupleIndex + 1], elements[tupleIndex + 2]);

      ReplaceOperation(elements, tupleIndex, newElement);
    }

    return (elements[0] as Operand).Value;
  }

  //

  private readonly Parser parser;

  private static int FindOperation(List<Element> elements)
  {
    for (var i = 0; i < elements.Count; i++)
      if (elements[i] is Operator)
        return i - 1;
```

## TDD by example – Evaluating an expression

```
        return 0;
    }

    private static Operand Compute(Element lOperand, Element op,
Element rOperand)
    {
        return new Operand((op as Operator).Compute(lOperand as
Operand, rOperand as Operand));
    }

    private static void ReplaceOperation(IList elements, int index,
Operand operand)
    {
      elements.RemoveAt(index + 2);
      elements.RemoveAt(index + 1);
      elements.RemoveAt(index);

      elements.Insert(index, operand);
    }
}
```

All tests pass except for the acceptance test, which fails with "Expected:<13>. Actual:<8>." – this means precedence is not respected, which I knew. However, left-to-right multiple operations work correctly. Good.

### 4.1. Smells-driven refactoring

TDD tends to highlight "pain points" in the code. If you ignore them, they multiply and soon testing becomes impossible. That is not a good idea.

There are also things in the code that you learn to be wary of as you program. Static methods, for example, sometimes signal that a new class should be created. So does the overuse of specific indexes (like "index + 2" above) or the overuse of casts.

I'll start by extracting the tuple into a separate class. I'll call this class Operation:

```csharp
public class Operation
{
  public Operand LOperand { get; private set; }
  public Operator Op { get; private set; }
  public Operand ROperand { get; private set; }

  public Operation(Operand lOperand, Operator op, Operand rOperand)
  {
    LOperand = lOperand;
    Op = op;
    ROperand = rOperand;
  }
}
```

The Evaluator class changes accordingly:

```csharp
public class Evaluator
{
  public Evaluator(Parser parser)
  {
    this.parser = parser;
  }

  public int Eval(string s)
  {
    if (string.IsNullOrEmpty(s))
      throw new Exception();

    var elements = parser.Parse(s).ToList();

    while (elements.Count > 1)
    {
      var tuple = FindOperation(elements);
      var newElement = Compute(tuple.Item2);

      ReplaceOperation(elements, tuple.Item1, newElement);
    }

    return (elements[0] as Operand).Value;
  }

  //

  private readonly Parser parser;
```

```
    private static Tuple<int, Operation>
FindOperation(List<Element> elements)
    {
       for (var i = 0; i < elements.Count; i++)
         if (elements[i] is Operator)
            return new Tuple<int, Operation>(i - 1, new
Operation(elements[i - 1] as Operand, elements[i] as Operator,
elements[i + 1] as Operand));

       return null;
    }

    private static Operand Compute(Operation operation)
    {
       return new Operand(operation.Op.Compute(operation.LOperand,
operation.ROperand));
    }

    private static void ReplaceOperation(IList elements, int index,
Operand operand)
    {
       elements.RemoveAt(index + 2);
       elements.RemoveAt(index + 1);
       elements.RemoveAt(index);

       elements.Insert(index, operand);
    }
 }
```

The Compute method screams to be moved to the Operation class:

```
    public Operand Compute()
    {
       return new Operand(Op.Compute(LOperand, ROperand));
    }
```

which means removing it from the Evaluator class and changing the Eval method:

```
    public int Eval(string s)
    {
      if (string.IsNullOrEmpty(s))
         throw new Exception();
```

```
    var elements = parser.Parse(s).ToList();

    while (elements.Count > 1)
    {
      var tuple = FindOperation(elements);
      var newElement = tuple.Item2.Compute();

      ReplaceOperation(elements, tuple.Item1, newElement);
    }

    return (elements[0] as Operand).Value;
}
```

Since the logic of the Operation.Compute method is very simple, I can ignore the lack of a test (I don't know what I would test anyway... I guess I could test that Op.Compute is being called, but I would have to make a lot of changes and I don't think the benefit justifies the cost).

Ok, all the tests, except for the acceptance test, are still passing. We're not done with the refactoring though.

### 4.2. Lists

Every time your program has a list of somethings, it's a good idea to ask yourself if it cannot be replaced by a custom class. The application will seldom need the whole power of List<T>, or T[], or whatever else you're using; in most cases you only need a few operations. Using a naked list leaks too much information and risks using too much internal knowledge where it shouldn't be used, which in turn makes the whole thing harder to change.

In this particular case, I'm using indices all over the place in the Eval method. The Eval method should not know about indices, or its knowledge should at least be limited. I should replace the List<Element> with an ElementList class. (Note that both the overuse of indices and the static methods suggest this change.)

How would the ElementList class be used? I don't need Count, IndexOf, RemoveAt or anything like that; I need FindOperation and ReplaceOperation methods. I'll start with the first:

```
[TestClass]
public class ElementListTests
{
  [TestMethod]
  public void FindOperationReturnsFirstOperation()
  {
    var lOperand = new Operand(0);
    var op = new AddOperator();
    var rOperand = new Operand(0);
    var sut = new ElementList(new Element[] { new Operand(0), new Operand(0), lOperand, op, rOperand });

    var result = sut.FindOperation();

    Assert.AreEqual(lOperand, result.LOperand);
    Assert.AreEqual(op, result.Op);
    Assert.AreEqual(rOperand, result.ROperand);
  }
}
```

Making the test compile is simple:

```
public class ElementList
{
  public ElementList(IList<Element> elements)
  {
    //
  }

  public Operation FindOperation()
  {
    return null;
  }
}
```

Making it pass is not that much harder, since I already have the method:

```
public class ElementList
{
  public ElementList(IList<Element> elements)
  {
    this.elements = elements;
  }

  public Operation FindOperation()
  {
    for (var i = 0; i < elements.Count; i++)
      if (elements[i] is Operator)
        return new Operation(elements[i - 1] as Operand, elements[i] as Operator, elements[i + 1] as Operand);

    return null;
  }

  //

  private readonly IList<Element> elements;
}
```

I don't return the index because I don't believe I need it anymore. Let's see if I am right:

```
[TestMethod]
public void ReplaceOperationReplacesTheCorrectOne()
{
  var otherOpd1 = new Operand(0);
  var otherOp = new AddOperator();
  var otherOpd2 = new Operand(0);
  var lOperand = new Operand(0);
  var op = new AddOperator();
  var rOperand = new Operand(0);
  var sut = new ElementList(new Element[] { otherOpd1, otherOp, otherOpd2, lOperand, op, rOperand });
  var operation = new Operation(lOperand, op, rOperand);

  sut.ReplaceOperation(operation, new Operand(0));

  // to confirm the replacement was correct, FindOperation should return the "other" one
```

```
        var result = sut.FindOperation();
        Assert.AreEqual(otherOpd1, result.LOperand);
        Assert.AreEqual(otherOp, result.Op);
        Assert.AreEqual(otherOpd2, result.ROperand);
    }
```

Making it compile:

```
    public void ReplaceOperation(Operation operation, Operand operand)
    {
        //
    }
```

Confirming that the test fails... oops. It doesn't.

I tried to be too clever. I foresaw a potential problem (what if the ReplaceOperation algorithm is incorrectly implemented, so that it always replaces the first operation it finds) and that's why I made the test change the second one. I'll disable this test for now using the [Ignore] attribute (I think it's a good test to have, after I have a working implementation) and add one that tests that ReplaceOperation works at all:

```
    [TestMethod]
    public void ReplaceOperationWorks()
    {
       var lOperand = new Operand(0);
       var op = new AddOperator();
       var rOperand = new Operand(0);
       var sut = new ElementList(new Element[] { lOperand, op, rOperand });
       var operation = new Operation(lOperand, op, rOperand);

       sut.ReplaceOperation(operation, new Operand(0));

       // FindOperation should return null now
       var result = sut.FindOperation();
       Assert.IsNull(result);
    }

    [TestMethod]
    [Ignore]
```

```csharp
public void ReplaceOperationReplacesTheCorrectOne()
{
   var otherOpd1 = new Operand(0);
   var otherOp = new AddOperator();
   var otherOpd2 = new Operand(0);
   var lOperand = new Operand(0);
   var op = new AddOperator();
   var rOperand = new Operand(0);
   var sut = new ElementList(new Element[] { otherOpd1, otherOp, otherOpd2, lOperand, op, rOperand });
   var operation = new Operation(lOperand, op, rOperand);

   sut.ReplaceOperation(operation, new Operand(0));

   // to confirm the replacement was correct, FindOperation should return the "other" one
   var result = sut.FindOperation();
   Assert.AreEqual(otherOpd1, result.LOperand);
   Assert.AreEqual(otherOp, result.Op);
   Assert.AreEqual(otherOpd2, result.ROperand);
}
```

The ReplaceOperationWorks test fails. Let's make it pass:

```csharp
public void ReplaceOperation(Operation operation, Operand operand)
{
   elements.RemoveAt(2);
   elements.RemoveAt(1);
   elements[0] = operand;
}
```

Running the test... it fails with "System.NotSupportedException: Collection was of a fixed size." Huh? Looking it up, it seems that the problem is that I'm assigning an array to an IList and an array cannot change size.

Oh well, I was worried about changing the list I got injected into the constructor anyway. Let's change the constructor to make this work:

```csharp
public ElementList(IEnumerable<Element> elements)
{
   this.elements = new List<Element>(elements);
```

}

Now the test passes. Good, let me re-enable the test I disabled and see what happens. It fails with a not very clear message ("Assert.AreEqual failed. Expected:<Renfield.Math.ExpressionEvaluator.Operand>. Actual:<Renfield.Math.ExpressionEvaluator.Operand>.") but at least it fails where expected. It can be made to pass:

```
    public void ReplaceOperation(Operation operation, Operand operand)
    {
      var index = elements.IndexOf(operation.LOperand);

      elements.RemoveAt(index + 2);
      elements.RemoveAt(index + 1);
      elements[index] = operand;
    }
```

I can now go back to the Evaluator.Eval method:

```
    public class Evaluator
    {
      public Evaluator(Parser parser)
      {
        this.parser = parser;
      }

      public int Eval(string s)
      {
        if (string.IsNullOrEmpty(s))
          throw new Exception();

        var elements = new ElementList(parser.Parse(s));

        var operation = elements.FindOperation();
        while (operation != null)
        {
          var newElement = operation.Compute();
          elements.ReplaceOperation(operation, newElement);

          operation = elements.FindOperation();
        }
```

```
        return elements.First.Value;
    }

    //

    private readonly Parser parser;
}
```

I had to add a First property to the ElementList class, so I'll write a test for it:

```
[TestMethod]
public void FirstReturnsFirstElement()
{
    var lOperand = new Operand(0);
    var op = new AddOperator();
    var rOperand = new Operand(0);
    var sut = new ElementList(new Element[] { lOperand, op, rOperand });

    var result = sut.First;

    Assert.AreEqual(lOperand, result);
}
```

Making it compile:

```
public Operand First
{
    get { return null; }
}
```

Whoa... I just broke everything (only 19 tests pass, 14 fail). Quickly, let's fix that:

```
public Operand First
{
    get { return elements[0] as Operand; }
}
```

Whew.

The refactoring was so far a success... partially, at least. I don't like the "feature envy" smell I can see in the Eval method –

most of its logic asks an ElementList for something, processes that something and then sends the result back to the ElementList. It strongly looks like the whole thing should be inside ElementList, but then I'd have just renamed the Evaluator class to ElementList. I guess I prefer keeping the list management and the expression evaluation logic in two separate classes, so it stays like this for now.

## 4.3. Operator precedence

It's time to bite the bullet and fix the last acceptance test. I'll start with a unit test in the EvaluatorTests class:

```
[TestMethod]
public void TwoOperationsRespectingPrecedence()
{
  CheckEvaluation("2+3*5", 17);
}
```

This fails with the message "Expected:<17>. Actual:<25>."

How do I fix it? I need to add a new property to the Operator class. I haven't needed an OperatorTests class yet so I'll add one:

```
[TestClass]
public class OperatorTests
{
  [TestMethod]
  public void AddOperatorPrecedenceIsSetCorrectly()
  {
    var sut = new AddOperator();

    Assert.AreEqual(1, sut.Precedence);
  }
}
```

Since the Operator class itself is abstract, I can't create an instance, but I consider these to be generic Operator tests so I won't move them to the AddOperatorTests class.

The change to the Operator class is easy to make:

```
public abstract class Operator : Element
{
  public int Precedence { get; protected set; }

  public abstract int Compute(Operand left, Operand right);
}
```

The test fails, so I need to add a constructor to make it pass:

```
public AddOperator()
{
  Precedence = 1;
}
```

The test passes. I'll add the other three tests in the same method (and rename it):

```
[TestMethod]
public void OperatorPrecedenceIsSetCorrectly()
{
  Assert.AreEqual(1, new AddOperator().Precedence);
  Assert.AreEqual(1, new SubOperator().Precedence);
  Assert.AreEqual(2, new MulOperator().Precedence);
  Assert.AreEqual(2, new DivOperator().Precedence);
}
```

The changes are trivial:

```
public SubOperator()
{
  Precedence = 1;
}

public MulOperator()
{
  Precedence = 2;
}

public DivOperator()
{
  Precedence = 2;
}
```

The tests pass now – I still have the acceptance test and the new Evaluator unit test failing, of course. To fix that, the FindOperation method needs to return the first operation with the highest precedence; that's a new test in the ElementListTests class:

```
[TestMethod]
public void FindOperationReturnsHighestPrecedence()
{
    var lOperand = new Operand(0);
    var op = new MulOperator();
    var rOperand = new Operand(0);
    var sut = new ElementList(new Element[] { new Operand(0), new AddOperator(), new Operand(0), lOperand, op, rOperand });

    var result = sut.FindOperation();

    Assert.AreEqual(lOperand, result.LOperand);
    Assert.AreEqual(op, result.Op);
    Assert.AreEqual(rOperand, result.ROperand);
}
```

The test fails, as expected. Let's fix it:

```
public Operation FindOperation()
{
    var operators = elements.Where(el => el is Operator).Cast<Operator>();
    if (!operators.Any())
        return null;

    // I don't know if OrderByDescending is stable so I won't use that
    var maxPrecedence = operators.Max(op => op.Precedence);
    var firstOp = operators.First(op => op.Precedence == maxPrecedence);

    var index = elements.IndexOf(firstOp);
    return new Operation(elements[index - 1] as Operand, elements[index] as Operator, elements[index + 1] as Operand);
}
```

All tests are passing; the evaluator is now respecting operator precedence.

## Chapter 5. More complex expressions

I need to add support for parentheses; also, since I've never used them before, I'll add some negative numbers in the mix:

```
[TestMethod]
public void ComplexExpression()
{
    CheckEvaluation("-2+3*(-5+8-9)/2", -11);
}
```

The test fails. I'll start fixing that with handling negative numbers.

### 5.1. Negative numbers

There is a problem with the way I'm identifying operations: I'm assuming that an operator is binary (it has operands on both sides). However, negative numbers use a unary operator – it only has an operand on the right side. Let's expose that problem with a test:

```
[TestMethod]
public void NegativeNumber()
{
    CheckEvaluation("-3", -3);
}
```

It fails... inside the parser. I didn't realize that, but the parser can't handle a non-empty string that nevertheless doesn't start with a digit:

```
[TestMethod]
public void NegativeNumber()
{
    var sut = new Parser(new OperatorFactory(), new OperandFactory());

    var result = sut.Parse("-3").ToList();

    Assert.AreEqual(2, result.Count);
    Assert.IsInstanceOfType(result[0], typeof (SubOperator));
```

```
    Assert.AreEqual(3, ((Operand) result[1]).Value);
}
```

The test fails as expected. Fixing it is simple:

```
public IEnumerable<Element> Parse(string s)
{
  var operand = "";
  foreach (var currentChar in s)
  {
    if (char.IsDigit(currentChar))
      operand += currentChar;
    else
    {
      if (operand != "")
        yield return
operandFactory.Create(Convert.ToInt32(operand));
      operand = "";

      yield return operatorFactory.Create(currentChar);
    }
  }

  if (operand != "")
    yield return
operandFactory.Create(Convert.ToInt32(operand));
}
```

The test passes. I fixed the Parser class; now the ElementList class has a problem – FindOperation throws because of the missing operand to the left. I'll expose the problem with a test:

```
[TestMethod]
public void FindOperationCanHandleNegativeNumbers()
{
  var op = new SubOperator();
  var rOperand = new Operand(1);
  var sut = new ElementList(new Element[] { op, rOperand });

  var result = sut.FindOperation();

  Assert.IsNull(result.LOperand);
  Assert.AreEqual(op, result.Op);
  Assert.AreEqual(rOperand, result.ROperand);
}
```

Fixing it means treating the case where the index is out of range:

```
    public Operation FindOperation()
    {
       var operators = elements.Where(el => el is
Operator).Cast<Operator>();
       if (!operators.Any())
         return null;

       // I don't know if OrderByDescending is stable so I won't use
that
       var maxPrecedence = operators.Max(op => op.Precedence);
       var firstOp = operators.First(op => op.Precedence ==
maxPrecedence);

       var index = elements.IndexOf(firstOp);
       return new Operation(GetOperand(index - 1), elements[index]
as Operator, GetOperand(index + 1));
    }

    private Operand GetOperand(int index)
    {
       return index < 0 || index >= elements.Count
             ? null
             : elements[index] as Operand;
    }
```

The EvaluatorTests.NegativeNumber test is still failing, however... because the SubOperator.Compute method expects a non-null left operand. I think it would be better to return a zero instead of a null operand, so I'll change the ElementListTests test:

```
    [TestMethod]
    public void FindOperationCanHandleNegativeNumbers()
    {
      var op = new SubOperator();
      var rOperand = new Operand(1);
      var sut = new ElementList(new Element[] { op, rOperand });

      var result = sut.FindOperation();
```

```
Assert.AreEqual(0, result.LOperand.Value);
Assert.AreEqual(op, result.Op);
Assert.AreEqual(rOperand, result.ROperand);
}
```

Fixing it is simple:

```
private Operand GetOperand(int index)
{
  return index < 0 || index >= elements.Count
          ? new Operand(0)
          : elements[index] as Operand;
}
```

This test passes, but the NegativeNumber test is still failing – this time because of the ReplaceOperation method. I'll write a test for it:

```
[TestMethod]
public void ReplaceOperationCanHandleNegativeNumbers()
{
  var op = new SubOperator();
  var rOperand = new Operand(1);
  var sut = new ElementList(new Element[] { op, rOperand });
  var operation = sut.FindOperation();

  sut.ReplaceOperation(operation, new Operand(-1));

  Assert.AreEqual(-1, sut.First.Value);
  Assert.IsNull(sut.FindOperation());
}
```

The test fails because the ReplaceOperation method wants to delete the left operand too, not to mention it's trying to find the operation by looking for the left operand (and not finding it). I'll fix it:

```
public void ReplaceOperation(Operation operation, Operand operand)
    {
    var index = elements.IndexOf(operation.Op);

    if (GetOperand(index + 1) == operation.ROperand)
      elements.RemoveAt(index + 1);
```

```
        elements[index] = operand;
        if (GetOperand(index - 1) == operation.LOperand)
            elements.RemoveAt(index - 1);
    }
```

(Note, again, that I'm changing the code in small increments and it only takes a minute to do so.)

All the tests, except for the acceptance test, are now passing.

## 5.2. Parentheses

I'll start with a simple case, a number within parentheses:

```
[TestMethod]
public void NumberInParentheses()
{
    CheckEvaluation("(3)", 3);
}
```

The test fails with the message "Unknown operator [(]", because the parser sees a non-digit character and assumes it's an operator. I could add a new type inheriting from Element (or two – for open and closed parentheses) but I prefer another way of dealing with this: I'll use a "precedence booster" that increases by 10 every time I encounter an open parenthesis and decreases by 10 for every closing parenthesis. Each time I find an operator, add the value of the booster to the default precedence of the operator. (This algorithm also has the benefit that I can easily detect unbalanced parentheses – if the booster is not zero at the end, something is wrong.)

The change has to be made inside the parser. I start by adding a test to the ParserTests class just to confirm that it doesn't break on parentheses:

```
[TestMethod]
public void NumberInParentheses()
{
```

```
    var sut = new Parser(new OperatorFactory(), new
OperandFactory());

    var result = sut.Parse("(3)").ToList();

    Assert.AreEqual(1, result.Count);
    Assert.AreEqual(3, ((Operand) result[0]).Value);
}
```

I'll fix it in the simplest way, by ignoring the open/closing parentheses:

```
    public IEnumerable<Element> Parse(string s)
    {
      var operand = "";
      foreach (var currentChar in s)
      {
        if (char.IsDigit(currentChar))
          operand += currentChar;
        else
        {
          if (operand != "")
            yield return
operandFactory.Create(Convert.ToInt32(operand));
          operand = "";

          if (currentChar != '(' && currentChar != ')')
            yield return operatorFactory.Create(currentChar);
        }
      }
      if (operand != "")
        yield return
operandFactory.Create(Convert.ToInt32(operand));
    }
```

I'm a bit surprised – all the tests pass except for the acceptance test.

Time for a short break – I'll extract the creation of the parser into a private method; all tests except for the second one (ParseCallsOperandFactoryCreate) will use this method:

```
    private static Parser CreateParser()
```

```
    {
        return new Parser(new OperatorFactory(), new
OperandFactory());
    }
```

The same tests still pass, so I didn't break anything. Ok, I need a parser test to handle the precedence boost:

```
[TestMethod]
public void OperatorsInParenthesesGetAPrecedenceBoost()
{
   var sut = CreateParser();

   var result = sut.Parse("(1+2)").ToList();

   Assert.AreEqual(3, result.Count);
   Assert.AreEqual(1, ((Operand) result[0]).Value);
   Assert.AreEqual(11, ((Operator) result[1]).Precedence);
   Assert.AreEqual(2, ((Operand) result[2]).Value);
}
```

This test fails, predictably, with "Expected:<11>. Actual:<1>." Fixing it will require several changes, beginning with the Parse method:

```
public IEnumerable<Element> Parse(string s)
{
   const int BOOST = 10;

   var precedenceBoost = 0;

   var operand = "";
   foreach (var currentChar in s)
   {
      if (char.IsDigit(currentChar))
         operand += currentChar;
      else
      {
         if (operand != "")
            yield return
operandFactory.Create(Convert.ToInt32(operand));
         operand = "";

         if (currentChar == '(')
            precedenceBoost += BOOST;
```

## TDD by example – Evaluating an expression

```
    var sut = new Parser(new OperatorFactory(), new
OperandFactory());

    var result = sut.Parse("(3)").ToList();

    Assert.AreEqual(1, result.Count);
    Assert.AreEqual(3, ((Operand) result[0]).Value);
}
```

I'll fix it in the simplest way, by ignoring the open/closing parentheses:

```
public IEnumerable<Element> Parse(string s)
{
  var operand = "";
  foreach (var currentChar in s)
  {
    if (char.IsDigit(currentChar))
      operand += currentChar;
    else
    {
      if (operand != "")
        yield return
operandFactory.Create(Convert.ToInt32(operand));
      operand = "";

      if (currentChar != '(' && currentChar != ')')
        yield return operatorFactory.Create(currentChar);
    }
  }

  if (operand != "")
    yield return
operandFactory.Create(Convert.ToInt32(operand));
}
```

I'm a bit surprised – all the tests pass except for the acceptance test.

Time for a short break – I'll extract the creation of the parser into a private method; all tests except for the second one (ParseCallsOperandFactoryCreate) will use this method:

```
private static Parser CreateParser()
```

```
    {
        return new Parser(new OperatorFactory(), new
OperandFactory());
    }
```

The same tests still pass, so I didn't break anything. Ok, I need a parser test to handle the precedence boost:

```
    [TestMethod]
    public void OperatorsInParenthesesGetAPrecedenceBoost()
    {
        var sut = CreateParser();

        var result = sut.Parse("(1+2)").ToList();

        Assert.AreEqual(3, result.Count);
        Assert.AreEqual(1, ((Operand) result[0]).Value);
        Assert.AreEqual(11, ((Operator) result[1]).Precedence);
        Assert.AreEqual(2, ((Operand) result[2]).Value);
    }
```

This test fails, predictably, with "Expected:<11>. Actual:<1>." Fixing it will require several changes, beginning with the Parse method:

```
    public IEnumerable<Element> Parse(string s)
    {
        const int BOOST = 10;

        var precedenceBoost = 0;

        var operand = "";
        foreach (var currentChar in s)
        {
            if (char.IsDigit(currentChar))
                operand += currentChar;
            else
            {
                if (operand != "")
                    yield return
operandFactory.Create(Convert.ToInt32(operand));
                operand = "";

                if (currentChar == '(')
                    precedenceBoost += BOOST;
```

```
      else if (currentChar == ')')
        precedenceBoost -= BOOST;
      else
        yield return operatorFactory.Create(currentChar, precedenceBoost);
      }
    }

    if (operand != "")
      yield return
operandFactory.Create(Convert.ToInt32(operand));
  }
```

This doesn't compile because of the additional argument to the operatorFactory.Create call. I'll change the OperatorFactoryTests.Check private method to add the new parameter:

```
    private void Check(char op, Type type)
    {
      var result = sut.Create(op, 0);

      Assert.IsInstanceOfType(result, type);
    }
```

and then change the OperatorFactory.Create method:

```
    public Operator Create(char op, int precedenceBoost)
    {
      switch (op)
      {
        case '+':
          return new AddOperator(precedenceBoost);
        case '-':
          return new SubOperator(precedenceBoost);
        case '*':
          return new MulOperator(precedenceBoost);
        case '/':
          return new DivOperator(precedenceBoost);
        default:
          throw new Exception(string.Format("Unknown operator [{0}]", op));
      }
    }
```

This means changing all four operator classes; I'll add a new test to the AddOperatorTests class to show how the boost is taken into account:

```
[TestMethod]
public void TakesPrecedenceBoostIntoAccount()
{
    var sut = new AddOperator(7);
    Assert.AreEqual(8, sut.Precedence);
}
```

The change to the AddOperator class is simple:

```
public AddOperator(int precedenceBoost = 0)
{
    Precedence = 1 + precedenceBoost;
}
```

The changes to the other three operators (and the matching test classes) are similar so I'm not going to show them.

Everything compiles except for a test in the OperatorFactoryTests class; easily fixed:

```
[TestMethod]
[ExpectedException(typeof (Exception))]
public void UnknownSignThrowsException()
{
    sut.Create('x', 0);
}
```

All the tests pass except for the acceptance test, which complains about the negative number in parentheses. Good point – I need a new test for that in the EvaluatorTests class:

```
[TestMethod]
public void NegativeNumberInParentheses()
{
    CheckEvaluation("(-3)", -3);
}
```

Hmm... this one passes. Ok, a more complicated one:

```
[TestMethod]
public void AddANegativeNumberInParentheses()
{
   CheckEvaluation("2+(-3)", -1);
}
```

Ok, this one fails. The reason it fails is more subtle... the parser returns two successive operators and the FindOperation can't handle that. Let's expose the problem with a test in the ElementListTests class:

```
[TestMethod]
public void FindOperationCanHandleTwoSuccessiveOperators()
{
   var opd1 = new Operand(1);
   var op1 = new AddOperator();
   var op2 = new SubOperator(10);
   var opd2 = new Operand(2);
   var sut = new ElementList(new Element[] { opd1, op1, op2, opd2 });

   var result = sut.FindOperation();

   Assert.AreEqual(0, result.LOperand.Value);
   Assert.AreEqual(op2, result.Op);
   Assert.AreEqual(opd2, result.ROperand);
}
```

This fails with "Object reference not set to an instance of an object." on the first assert. Let's fix it:

```
private Operand GetOperand(int index)
{
    if (index >= 0 && index < elements.Count && elements[index] is Operand)
        return (Operand) elements[index];

    return new Operand(0);
}
```

Success – all the tests pass!

## 5.3. Refactoring

Minor cleanup for the ParserTests class – I want to include the Parse call and the parser creation in a single method:

```
private static List<Element> Parse(string s)
{
   var sut = new Parser(new OperatorFactory(), new OperandFactory());

   return sut.Parse(s).ToList();
}
```

The first test becomes:

```
[TestMethod]
public void ParseReturnsAdditionElements()
{
  var result = Parse("1+2");

  Assert.AreEqual(3, result.Count);
  Assert.IsInstanceOfType(result[0], typeof (Operand));
  Assert.IsInstanceOfType(result[1], typeof (Operator));
  Assert.IsInstanceOfType(result[2], typeof (Operand));
}
```

All the tests in the ParserTests class except for the second one change accordingly.

## Chapter 6. Floating-point numbers

One of the problems with the YAGNI mantra is that it will create some problems if you are, in fact, going to need it. Whether that is offset by the fact that it remains true in most cases is, of course, up to you.

> *YAGNI: You Ain't Gonna Need It – a principle of extreme programming which says that you should refrain from adding code to enable features that you know are going to be added at some point in the future. Wait until the customers are actually requesting those features – they might never do, or the features might be implemented in an unexpected way.*

In this particular case, I knew I was going to handle floating-point numbers eventually, but I chose not to complicate my code too soon – there was plenty of code to write even without adding that requirement. This is going to mean I need to change a lot of ints to doubles, and I will also need to pay attention to the Assert.AreEqual calls, since deciding the equality of floating-point numbers is a bit more complicated than that.

> *If you haven't encountered this before, floating-point operations have errors in most computer languages: 1 / 3 \* 3 will seldom be equal to 1. That being the case, the writers of the testing framework have added an additional "delta" (think of it as precision) parameter to the Assert.AreEqual call; instead of Assert.AreEqual(2.5, result) you will write Assert.AreEqual(2.5, result, 0.01), which means any value of result between 2.49 and 2.51 will be considered "equal enough".*

Ok. Let's write an acceptance test that uses floating point numbers; because this is an acceptance test, not a unit test (so it can check for multiple things), I'm also going to add a couple of levels of parentheses to see that the code handles them correctly:

```
[TestMethod]
public void ComplexExpressionWithFloatingPointNumbers()
{
   CheckEvaluation("1.2*6/(2.74-9.1*(-5.27)/(3+17.4*(9.15-1.225)))", 3.08, 0.01);
}
```

This means I need to change the CheckEvaluation method:

```
private static void CheckEvaluation(string s, double expected, double precision = 0.0001)
  {
     var parser = new Parser(new OperatorFactory(), new OperandFactory());
     var sut = new Evaluator(parser);

     var result = sut.Eval(s);

     Assert.AreEqual(expected, result, precision);
  }
```

Running the tests shows me that only the new one fails. I'll start changing the ints to doubles now. The first one is the Evaluator.Eval method (I'm not going to show it here, only the return type changes).

The next class to change is Operand:

```
public class Operand : Element
{
  public double Value { get; private set; }

  public Operand(double value)
  {
    Value = value;
  }
```

}

This one breaks the operators; let's change those classes too:

```
public abstract class Operator : Element
{
  public int Precedence { get; protected set; }

  public abstract double Compute(Operand left, Operand right);
}
public class AddOperator : Operator
{
  public AddOperator(int precedenceBoost = 0)
  {
    Precedence = 1 + precedenceBoost;
  }

  public override double Compute(Operand left, Operand right)
  {
    return left.Value + right.Value;
  }
}
```

(SubOperator, MulOperator and DivOperator change similarly.)

All the tests, except for the new acceptance test, still pass. Huh... this is less painful than I expected.

Ok, I'll start working on the actual requirement. First, a new test in the EvaluatorTests class:

```
[TestMethod]
public void FloatingPointNumber()
{
  CheckEvaluation("1.5", 1.5, 0.01);
}
```

The CheckEvaluation method will have to be changed too, just as the one in AcceptanceTests was:

```
    private static void CheckEvaluation(string s, double expected,
double precision = 0.0001)
    {
        var parser = new Parser(new OperatorFactory(), new
OperandFactory());
        var sut = new Evaluator(parser);

        var result = sut.Eval(s);

        Assert.AreEqual(expected, result, precision);
    }
```

The new unit test fails; there's nothing I can do about it here, it's a parsing issue, so here's the new parser test:

```
    [TestMethod]
    public void FloatingPointNumber()
    {
      var result = Parse("1.5");

      Assert.AreEqual(1, result.Count);
      Assert.AreEqual(1.5, ((Operand) result[0]).Value, 0.01);
    }
```

This test fails with the message "Unknown operator [.]" – ok, time to change the code:

```
    public IEnumerable<Element> Parse(string s)
    {
      const int BOOST = 10;

      var precedenceBoost = 0;

      var operand = "";
      foreach (var currentChar in s)
      {
        if (char.IsDigit(currentChar) || currentChar == '.')
          operand += currentChar;
        else
        {
          if (operand != "")
            yield return
operandFactory.Create(Convert.ToDouble(operand));
          operand = "";
```

```
        if (currentChar == '(')
          precedenceBoost += BOOST;
        else if (currentChar == ')')
          precedenceBoost -= BOOST;
        else
          yield return operatorFactory.Create(currentChar,
precedenceBoost);
      }
    }

    if (operand != "")
      yield return
operandFactory.Create(Convert.ToDouble(operand));
  }
```

This doesn't compile because of the operandFactory.Create call. Let's change the interface:

```
public interface IOperandFactory
{
  Operand Create(double value);
}
```

and the implementation:

```
public class OperandFactory : IOperandFactory
{
  public Operand Create(double value)
  {
    return new Operand(value);
  }
}
```

Let me make sure I have a test covering the change in the OperandFactoryTests class:

```
[TestMethod]
public void CreateReturnsOperandWithCorrectFloatingPointValue()
{
  var sut = new OperandFactory();

  var result = sut.Create(5.73);

  Assert.AreEqual(5.73, result.Value, 0.01);
}
```

This test passes. I'll take a short break to remove the duplication in this class, since I have code repeating three times:

```
[TestClass]
public class OperandFactoryTests
{
  [TestMethod]
  public void CreateReturnsOperand()
  {
    var result = GetOperand(5);

    Assert.IsInstanceOfType(result, typeof (Operand));
  }

  [TestMethod]
  public void CreateReturnsOperandWithCorrectValue()
  {
    var result = GetOperand(5);

    Assert.AreEqual(5, result.Value);
  }

  [TestMethod]
  public void CreateReturnsOperandWithCorrectFloatingPointValue()
  {
    var result = GetOperand(5.73);

    Assert.AreEqual(5.73, result.Value, 0.01);
  }

  //

  private static Operand GetOperand(double value)
  {
    var sut = new OperandFactory();

    return sut.Create(value);
  }
}
```

All the tests in this class pass. Running all the tests, I see that ParserTests. ParseCallsOperandFactoryCreate fails. Duh, it's still expecting an int, let me change that:

# TDD by example – Evaluating an expression

```
[TestMethod]
public void ParseCallsOperandFactoryCreate()
{
   var operandFactory = new Mock<IOperandFactory>();
   operandFactory
     .Setup(it => it.Create(It.IsAny<double>()))
     .Verifiable();

   var sut = new Parser(new OperatorFactory(), operandFactory.Object);

   sut.Parse("1").ToList();

   operandFactory.Verify();
}
```

All the tests pass, except for the acceptance test... which fails with the message "Expected a difference no greater than <0.01> between expected value <3.08> and actual value <2.33737848474675>." Hmm, I just wrote that expression and then pasted it into the Windows calculator but I forgot to press the "=" sign. Silly mistake; let me fix the acceptance test:

```
[TestMethod]
public void ComplexExpressionWithFloatingPointNumbers()
{
    CheckEvaluation("1.2*6/(2.74-9.1*(-5.27)/(3+17.4*(9.15-1.225)))", 2.33, 0.01);
}
```

All the tests pass. I keep getting surprised by how easy it is to change the code. I guess YAGNI was not as bad as I feared (in this case at least).

One refactoring remains to be done; I should use a switch statement instead of multiple ifs in the Parser.Parse method:

```
public IEnumerable<Element> Parse(string s)
{
   const int BOOST = 10;

   var precedenceBoost = 0;
```

```
      var operand = "";
      foreach (var currentChar in s)
      {
        if (char.IsDigit(currentChar) || currentChar == '.')
          operand += currentChar;
        else
        {
          if (operand != "")
            yield return
operandFactory.Create(Convert.ToDouble(operand));
          operand = "";

          switch (currentChar)
          {
            case '(':
              precedenceBoost += BOOST;
              break;

            case ')':
              precedenceBoost -= BOOST;
              break;

            default:
              yield return operatorFactory.Create(currentChar,
precedenceBoost);
              break;
          }
        }
      }

      if (operand != "")
        yield return
operandFactory.Create(Convert.ToDouble(operand));
    }
```

All the tests still pass.

## 6.1. Malformed expressions

There is a problem that lingers in the code: what happens with malformed expressions? Specifically, what happens with expressions with unbalanced parentheses and/or double decimal points inside a number? I think I should raise exceptions in these cases.

Since this is a parsing issue, I'll start by adding a test to the ParserTests class:

```
[TestMethod]
[ExpectedException(typeof (Exception))]
public void TooManyOpenParentheses()
{
   Parse("(1");
}
```

This test fails because the code did not throw an exception. Let me fix that:

```
public IEnumerable<Element> Parse(string s)
{
   const int BOOST = 10;

   var precedenceBoost = 0;

   var operand = "";
   foreach (var currentChar in s)
   {
     if (char.IsDigit(currentChar) || currentChar == '.')
       operand += currentChar;
     else
     {
       if (operand != "")
         yield return
operandFactory.Create(Convert.ToDouble(operand));
       operand = "";

       switch (currentChar)
       {
         case '(':
           precedenceBoost += BOOST;
           break;

         case ')':
           precedenceBoost -= BOOST;
           break;

         default:
```

```
            yield return operatorFactory.Create(currentChar,
precedenceBoost);
            break;
        }
      }
    }

    if (operand != "")
      yield return
operandFactory.Create(Convert.ToDouble(operand));

    if (precedenceBoost > 0)
      throw new Exception("Too many open parentheses");
}
```

The test passes; I'll add the one for the opposite case:

```
[TestMethod]
[ExpectedException(typeof(Exception))]
public void TooManyClosedParentheses()
{
   Parse("1)");
}
```

and the matching change in the Parse method:

```
if (precedenceBoost < 0)
   throw new Exception("Too many closed parentheses");
```

Both tests pass now. Let me add a test for the double decimal point:

```
[TestMethod]
[ExpectedException(typeof(Exception))]
public void DoubleDecimalPoint()
{
   Parse("1.5.7");
}
```

This test fails... in an unexpected way: "System.FormatException: Input string was not in a correct format."

Makes sense; the decimal points are added to the current operand, no matter how many of them are encountered, and this blows up when trying to convert it to a double. Decision time: do I absolutely want to detect the problem myself, when the second decimal point is encountered, or is this good enough? Given that my point here is to show the TDD process and not to create the world's best expression evaluator, I'll go with "good enough". The test still needs to be changed:

```
[TestMethod]
[ExpectedException(typeof (FormatException))]
public void DoubleDecimalPoint()
{
   Parse("1.5.7");
}
```

All the tests pass and I verified that I'm safe against malformed expressions.

## 6.2. Spaces

Unfortunately, I forgot something else... spaces in the string being parsed will blow up. To show that, I'm adding a test to the ParserTests class:

```
[TestMethod]
public void ExpressionWithSpaces()
{
   var result = Parse("1 + 2");

   Assert.AreEqual(3, result.Count);
}
```

However, this is very easy to fix; I just need to change the foreach:

```
   foreach (var currentChar in s.Where(c =>
!char.IsWhiteSpace(c)))
```

All the tests pass again.

## Chapter 7. Symbols

The evaluator is pretty complete right now. I want to add something I haven't seen done in other similar examples: symbolic operands, as in "a + 3". Of course, I'm going to need to pass a way to evaluate those symbols; I'll do that with a dictionary. Here's the new acceptance test:

```
[TestMethod]
public void ExpressionWithSymbols()
{
    CheckEvaluation("(x + 3) / (y + 5)", 2, 0.01, new Dictionary<string, double> { { "x", 7 }, { "y", 0 } });
}
```

The CheckEvaluation method changes accordingly:

```
private static void CheckEvaluation(string s, double expected, double precision = 0.0001, IDictionary<string, double> symbols = null)
{
    var parser = new Parser(new OperatorFactory(), new OperandFactory(), symbols);
    var sut = new Evaluator(parser);

    var result = sut.Eval(s);

    Assert.AreEqual(expected, result, precision);
}
```

As you can see, I've decided that the Parser class is the one that needs to know about the symbols; it will change them into operands so that the rest of the code will remain unchanged.

A new test in the ParserTests is required:

```
[TestMethod]
public void SymbolicExpression()
{
    var sut = new Parser(new OperatorFactory(), new OperandFactory(), new Dictionary<string, double> { { "x", 10 } });

    var result = sut.Parse("x").ToList();
```

```
    Assert.AreEqual(1, result.Count);
    Assert.AreEqual(10, ((Operand) result[0]).Value);
}
```

I change the Parse constructor to handle the new argument:

```
public Parser(OperatorFactory operatorFactory, IOperandFactory operandFactory, IDictionary<string, double> symbols = null)
{
   this.operatorFactory = operatorFactory;
   this.operandFactory = operandFactory;
}
```

The two new tests fail; the letters are considered (unknown) operators. Fixing that require a few more changes to the Parse class:

```
public class Parser
{
   public Parser(OperatorFactory operatorFactory, IOperandFactory operandFactory, IDictionary<string, double> symbols = null)
   {
      this.operatorFactory = operatorFactory;
      this.operandFactory = operandFactory;
      this.symbols = symbols;
   }

   public IEnumerable<Element> Parse(string s)
   {
      const int BOOST = 10;

      var precedenceBoost = 0;

      var operand = "";
      foreach (var currentChar in s.Where(c => !char.IsWhiteSpace(c)))
      {
         if (char.IsLetterOrDigit(currentChar) || currentChar == '.')
            operand += currentChar;
         else
         {
            if (operand != "")
```

```
            yield return
operandFactory.Create(GetOperand(operand));
          operand = "";

          switch (currentChar)
          {
            case '(':
              precedenceBoost += BOOST;
              break;

            case ')':
              precedenceBoost -= BOOST;
              break;

            default:
              yield return operatorFactory.Create(currentChar,
precedenceBoost);
              break;
          }
        }
      }

      if (operand != "")
        yield return operandFactory.Create(GetOperand(operand));

      if (precedenceBoost > 0)
        throw new Exception("Too many open parentheses");
      if (precedenceBoost < 0)
        throw new Exception("Too many closed parentheses");
    }

    //

    private readonly OperatorFactory operatorFactory;
    private readonly IOperandFactory operandFactory;
    private readonly IDictionary<string, double> symbols;

    private double GetOperand(string operand)
    {
      return char.IsLetter(operand.First())
            ? symbols[operand]
            : Convert.ToDouble(operand);
    }
```

As you can see, the first test changed from char.IsLetter to char.IsLetterOrDigit; also, the conversion of the operand variable to a double has been extracted to a private method, which looks up the string in the symbols dictionary if it starts with a letter.

All the tests pass... and the expression evaluator class is complete (which simply means that I don't have any other requirements right now).

## Chapter 8. Conclusion

I hope the time spent on this was useful – not so much in learning how to evaluate an expression, but rather in learning how to develop an application by writing tests (executable specifications) before writing production code.

Whether you liked the book or not, please leave a review. The book will be freely available in several formats at the http://renfieldsoftware.com site; I would very much appreciate it if you shared it with friends or colleagues who might find it useful. It should also be available as a Kindle ebook on Amazon; please leave a review there if you can, it helps.

Thank you for taking the time to read this; I hope you enjoyed it.

## ABOUT THE AUTHOR

Marcel Popescu discovered computers when he was twelve years old. (According to his daughters, dinosaurs were still alive back then.) It was the first time he did not abandon a hobby and he's still unable to escape the thrill of writing code. He has worked with languages ranging from COBOL and FORTRAN to JavaScript, but right now his favorite language is C#.